PENGUIN BOOKS

Beyond Heart Mountain

Lee Ann Roripaugh was born and raised in Laramie,
Wyoming. She received an M.F.A. in creative writing
from Indiana University, where she taught as an associate
instructor. Other degrees include an M.M. in music
history from Indiana University and a B.M. in piano
performance from Indiana University. Ms. Roripaugh was
the winner of the Randall Jarrell International Poetry
Prize in 1995. Other honors include an AWP Intro
Award and an Academy of American Poets Prize. Her
work has appeared in journals such as *Parnassus: Poetry
in Review, New England Review, Black Warrior Review,
Cream City Review, Crab Orchard Review, Phoebe,* and
Seneca Review, among others. Her poetry has also been
selected for inclusion in the anthology *American Identities:
Contemporary Multicultural Voices,* as well as the Dell
anthology *Waltzing on Water: Poetry by Women.* Ms.
Roripaugh currently resides in Columbus, Ohio.

THE NATIONAL POETRY SERIES

The National Poetry Series was established in 1978 to ensure the publication of five poetry collections annually through participating publishers. The manuscripts are selected by five poets of national reputation. Publication is funded by James A. Michener, the Copernicus Society of America, Edward J. Piszek, the Lannan Foundation, and the Tiny Tiger Foundation.

1998 COMPETITION WINNERS

Rigoberto Gonzalez of New Mexico, *So Often the Pitcher Goes to Water Until It Breaks*
Chosen by Ai, to be published by University of Illinois Press

Harry Humes of Pennsylvania, *Ghost Pain*
Chosen by Pattiann Rogers, to be published by Milkweed Editions

Joan Murray of New York, *Looking for the Parade*
Chosen by Robert Bly, to be published by W. W. Norton

Ed Roberson of New Jersey, *Atmosphere Conditions*
Chosen by Nathaniel Mackey, to be published by Sun & Moon Press

Lee Ann Roripaugh of Ohio, *Beyond Heart Mountain*
Chosen by Ishmael Reed, to be published by Viking Penguin

LEE ANN RORIPAUGH

Beyond

Heart Mountain

PENGUIN BOOKS

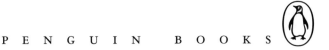

PENGUIN BOOKS
Published by the Penguin Group
Penguin Putnam Inc., 375 Hudson Street,
New York, New York 10014, U.S.A.
Penguin Books Ltd, 27 Wrights Lane,
London W8 5TZ, England
Penguin Books Australia Ltd, Ringwood,
Victoria, Australia
Penguin Books Canada Ltd, 10 Alcorn Avenue,
Toronto, Ontario, Canada M4V 3B2
Penguin Books (N.Z.) Ltd, 182-190 Wairau Road,
Auckland 10, New Zealand

Penguin Books Ltd, Registered Offices:
Harmondsworth, Middlesex, England

First published in Penguin Books 1999

1 2 3 4 5 6 7 8 9 10

LIBRARY OF CONGRESS IN PUBLICATION DATA
Roripaugh, Lee Ann.
    Beyond heart mountain/Lee Ann Roripaugh.
        p.   cm.—(National poetry series)
    ISBN 0-14-058920-1
    1. Japanese-Americans—Evacuations and relocation, 1942-1945—
Poetry.   2. World War, 1939-1945—Concentration camps—Wyoming—
Poetry.   3. Heart Mountain Relocation Center, Wyoming—Poetry.
I. Title.   II. Series.
PS3568.O717H4   1999
811'.54—dc21   98-47428

Printed in the United States of America
Set in Bembo
Designed by Mia Risberg

For my mother,

Yoshiko H. Roripaugh,

and my father,

Robert A. Roripaugh,

with love and gratitude.

CONTENTS

Part 1

Pearls	3
Ningyo	5
Chrysanthemums	8
Mitten Springs	11
I. Benny's Place	11
II. Antelope Hunting	12
III. Gutting	14
Coyote	16
Peach Girl	17
Oyurushi	18
Squid	19
A Dance of Wooden Shoes	20
Hiroshima Maiden	22

Part 2

Heart Mountain, 1943	27
I. Kimiko Ozawa	27
II. Jimmy Yamamoto	29
III. Masa Nakahara	31
IV. Chester Korematsu	33
V. Lily Iwasaki	35
VI. Sam Toyama	37
VII. Nina Inoue	39

VIII. *Yoshio Miyake*   41
IX. *Chikako Okano*   43
X. *Minoru Saito*   45

Part 3

Songs for an Approaching Rainy Season   49
The Woman Who Loves Insects   53
Star Festival   55
     I. *Sumida River*   55
     II. *Orihime's Song*   55
     III. *A Thousand Cranes*   56
Peony Lantern   57
Utoyasukata   59
Peony Lover   60
Ode to Sushi   62
Fish Wife   64
Kakitsubata   67

Acknowledgments   70

Part 1

PEARLS

Mother eats seaweed and plum pickles,
and when the Mormons come knocking
she does bird-talk. I've never seen
an ocean, but I'd swim in one to look
for secrets. She has a big pearl
from my oji-san, says it will be mine
when she's dead. It's in a drawer
hidden with silver dollars. I hope
she doesn't buy a ticket, go back
to her sisters and leave me.

With stinging strokes, she brushes
my hair, pulls it into pigtails
that stretch my face flat. I walk
to school across sagebrush while
she watches from her bedroom window.
Once I found a prairie dog curled
sleeping on the ground and I brushed
away ants on his eyes. Mother
saw me dilly-dally, told me not
to touch dead things.

I have a red box in my desk
with a dragon lid that screws on
and off. It smells sweet from face
cream and I keep a kokeishi doll
inside for good luck. Wishing
for more colors in my crayon pail,
I make up stories about mermaids
and want a gold crayon to draw hair,
silver for their tails. But
we can't afford lots of kid junk.

I have piano lessons. She says
I'll be a doctor someday
but I think I'd like to be a fireman
or maybe a roller derby queen.

One day when I was walking home
some boys on bikes flew down
around me like noisy crows.
They kept yelling *Kill the Jap!*
I ran fast as I could but fell
in the dirt, got up and fell.
My mother came running to me.
She carried me home, picked out
the gravel, washed off blood,
tucked me into her bed and let
me wear the ring for awhile.

I wish I had long, white skinny
fingers, gold hair and a silver
tail. I'd gather baskets
of pearls. But my hair is black,
my fingers stubby. Mother
tells me they're not found just
floating underwater. She says
oysters make them, when there's
sand or gravel under their shells.
It hurts. And the more it hurts,
the bigger the pearl.

NINGYO

I.

She took me everywhere
in my crocheted
lace dresses,
embroidered initials.
It pleased her
I could say
hippopotamus
so I said it
in the supermarket.
After hot baths,
laid out on the counter,
my hair floating
in the sink
like seaweed,
she would hand me
a mirror. *See?*
Tako-chan, the octopus
has left his ink.
I had a Japanese doll,
a snow queen
in a glass case
I couldn't touch.
I named her Yoshiko,
my mother's name.
Sometimes
when she was sleeping,
I pried
her eyelids open,
to make sure
she wasn't dead.

II.

I was angry we ate
Ramen every night.
She wouldn't let me
shave my legs,
and my grandparents
were stern pictures
wrapped in rice paper.
She said I gave her
high blood pressure,
and I felt
she was cold
as Yoshiko.

III.

My father bought me
an orange hat,
vest, earplugs,
a cheesecloth
for the carcass.
She packed up obento,
a coolerful
of Tab and beer.
We got to Shirley Basin
before dawn, gutting
my antelope by noon.
Some drunk men
drove by in a pickup
and yelled, *Goddamn,
it's a girl.* Circling
the prairie he told me,
*There are things
you don't understand.*

That night we cooked
over a kerosene stove
and drank Coors.
As I lay awake,
I could see a woman
who married an enemy
soldier. The frost
began to glisten
on my sleeping bag.
Stars, an eyelid
opening the sky.

CHRYSANTHEMUMS

Miss Yamada knew if a girl was tall and thin, or short and plump, by the sound of her voice, and she also knew if a girl was hiding a piece of candy in her mouth. This is what oka-san said. I worried Miss Yamada was some kind of oni, a devil, with eyeballs peering out from inside her ears and nostrils, blinking on her fingertips. She lived with her mother and never left the house. My sisters and I were all frightened of Miss Yamada's mother—balding and stooped, she did all of her shopping and errands in dark, old-fashioned kimonos, and geta shoes that made a hollow clop-clop sound as she walked. But Miss Yamada turned out to be delicate and quiet, with milky-white skin and cool fingers like weeping willow leaves. As she leaned over the koto, the back of her neck, in between wisps of black hair and the curving lip of her pale blue kimono, gave off a sweet, powdery scent from the rice talcum she used. She was like the women in wood-block prints—except for her eyes, which were cloudy like old tea that has been left in the pot for too long. Her voice held no sharp edges, but it had the same effect on me as listening to a shakuhachi flute—a kind of music that makes you feel sad inside. I fell in love with her. Sometimes I imagined Miss Yamada unpinning her hair at night, heavy black folds unfurling down to her waist. I longed to stand behind her and brush her hair, one hundred strokes, the way my mother sometimes let me do. I wished that I were a boy, so I could grow up and marry Miss Yamada.

I used to wait in her garden until it was time for my koto lesson. One day I was waiting for a long time, and I began to have a hot, ugly feeling inside—like a dragon blowing smoke inside my stomach. Miss Yamada was inside her house with Natsu Matsumoru. Was she feeding Natsu the rice candies she sometimes gave to me at the end of a lesson? Had she forgotten all about me? The garden was filled with chrysanthemums—explosions of color and petals that reminded me of the fireworks over Sumida River during Star Festival. And while I sat there with this bad feeling inside, they kept watching me, nodding at me on their stems, laughing at me until I couldn't stand it anymore and began to pick them—carelessly tearing them off, the ragged stems oozing single, clear drops.

I kept a red one to wear in my hair, and the rest I dismembered over by the pond, pulling off the petals one by one, chanting She Loves Me, She Loves Me Not. It was filled with giant, fan-tailed goldfish—mottled orange, red, and white, colored like the marbles my brothers sometimes played with. Some of them had puffy, exploded heads. I was afraid of these kind of goldfish because my mother had told me this was what happened to girls with tonkachi heads who didn't listen to their mothers. Soon the pond was filled with chrysanthemum petals, swirling in gentle whirlwinds around the shining bodies and dancing fan-tails of the agitated goldfish. Miss Yamada is blind, I kept saying to myself. She will not know that I have picked her chrysanthemums. But then I heard the shoji screen to the garden slide open, heard her call for me. I walked into the house with my heart loud as taiko drums. *I see that you are wearing a chrysanthemum corsage today.* This is what she said to me.

But this was years ago—before the war, before my koto was wrapped in silk and put in storage, before my father moved us up to the mountain house to protect us from the bombs. The day after the B-29 bombers flew over Ota City my brothers and sisters and I rode down from the mountain on our bicycles to see if our house was still standing. It was, but on our way there, we saw many others that were not—people searching rubble for belongings, relatives. This is when I rode my bicycle as fast as I could to Miss Yamada—pedaling, pedaling, out of breath. Her house was gone. The garden gone. And in front of where the house used to be, Miss Yamada's mother was screaming. The neighbors were trying to take something away from her. And even though it was burnt, blackened, the long fingers crushed, I saw whose hand it was before my eldest brother found me and dragged me away.

Today the American man with the gentle eyes, the big nose that he is always putting inside a book, has left chrysanthemums on my typewriter at the American occupation camp where I work. He is not like the others—he tosses rubber bands into my hair instead of trying to put his hand around my waist, and he shows me how to spell the long American words that I have to type all day without understanding what they mean. I hold the chrysanthemums up to my face and breathe in their tangy, pungent scent. Suddenly, I can see everything. Petals raining down to the bottom of Miss Yamada's goldfish pond. He Loves Me, He Loves Me Not. The smell so strong it makes my eyes sting. These chrysanthemums stolen, crossing an ocean to return them.

MITTEN SPRINGS

I. Benny's Place

We made camp
by the springs,
and my father
took me to Benny's—
Basque shepherd,
grandfather's friend.
His small cabin
lonely in so much sky
and sagebrush.
Three Ford trucks
by the fence,
all blue,
viny hops curling
up to the roofs.
His cot in a corner,
branding irons
on the walls,
tin cups and plates
in the kitchen.
Ducking through
the back door,
he spoke of a miracle,
and showed us
a sweetwater pond
where his garden
used to be,
split open by
a freak earthquake
and filled from
underground springs.

Brown trout
heard his voice
and began to spiral
toward the surface—
jostling into
one another,
a glimpse
of rolling fish-eye,
tortoise-shell bodies
shining and fat.
We fed them homemade Basque
bread, hard chunks
torn off black loaves,
and they leaped
like Spanish roses
flung from the snow.

II. Antelope Hunting

Stirring up grouse,
pungent scent
of crushed sage,
my sleepy footsteps
stumbled behind my father's.
Nudging gray puffballs
with the toe
of my boot,
mushroom-shaped clouds
of spores floated up.
As we climbed
into basins,
the rims cupped us
like earthenware bowls—
the sky so empty
I knew it could

drink me. Crawling
up each ridge
to look into
the next basin:
grit in my mouth,
sting of cacti.
On my belly
I saw the beetle's
obsidian sparkle.
Ants dragged
a grasshopper through
dust and quartz.
When my father
whispered *This is it,*
a stream of tan and white
spilled into the basin,
nostrils steaming.
We circled the rim
to get downwind,
then ran in a crouch,
and he pointed out
the buck—his, the one
who had called to him
from beyond
the next ridge
all morning.
I was fourteen, cradled
in my father's arms
against the recoil,
against the explosion
of dust and hoofbeats.

III. *Gutting*

Sawing the ribcage
was hard work.
Cut too deep
and there's a sudden
hiss, stench,
overflow of brilliant,
sage-flecked insides
steaming the autumn air.
A blue-veined maze
of intestines—
I lifted them out,
unraveling—lungs,
an elegant pink froth.
I rinsed the cavity
clean, vault
of hollowed ribcage
the ceiling arch
of a Gothic cathedral,
and wrapped the body
in cheesecloth
for the long ride home.
Transplanted
into the ice chest,
the heart soaked
in cold salt water,
beating against
the galvanized pail
with each dusty
bump of road.
Next morning
my father showed me
how to roll it
in peppered flour,
cook it in a frying pan.

We ate for something
more than hunger—
tough to chew, I let
the spicy sage taste
run through me.

We spotted him scouting antelope along Bison Basin Road, like a pale, gold flicker out of the frostbitten sage. He was dancing through the rifle scopes—body arching into the air like a flame, whip of a long, plumed tail. A slender muzzle shooting towards sky, neck muscles straining, until the steel trap on his hind leg snapped him down to the ground like a wet dishrag. Then, tail lowered, he panted, steamy breath camouflaging into the dust clouds that came to rest beside him. He didn't make a sound. In town, a man kept coyotes in his back yard. They stared at visitors with yellow eyes, slipping in and out of their underground dens, howling in counterpoint to fire trucks and police cars. My father and I raised our rifles—deep breath in, the slow squeeze of trigger. Then I held him and stroked crimson-tipped fur, his silky pointed ears, a glimpse of ivory bone where he was chewing off his leg . . . held him, until the curve of his ribs began to cool beneath my fingers.

PEACH GIRL

Apprehended by snow,
barbed-wire cattle fences
in the shadow of Heart Mountain,
the wrecker pulled
my giant peach
of an airport shuttle down
the highway and I rode inside,
secure as a thumb.
I returned to this irony
ripe for the plucking—
your mouth grazing
the fragrance of my skin.
Nectar, cleft and hollow,
the sublimation of blood
warming to sweetness—
the way ice melts
and begins to trickle
down the mountain pass
during spring's thaw.
But the soil here
is too cold and dry
for my shy seed of heart,
and you will never know
my peach blossoms.
When you eat the forbidden,
sooner or later your teeth
scrape against stone, bitter,
and you will spit it out.

OYURUSHI

We danced hopscotch squares,
pricked our fingers, blood sisters.
Hiding in the bathroom at recess,
we ate Jell-O chocolate pudding mix
and licked clean each other's hands.
She hid her mother's perfume in a lunch-
box, dabbed it behind my ears, then
gave me a paper cube with a peephole—
I looked inside and saw
You are my best friend.

The other girls taunted us.
She clung to me as I struggled
to pry each finger loose
until I tore away her sweaty palm.
I could not meet her antelope eyes
as she played alone, black hair
leaping the rigid arrow of her back.
She folded another paper cube—
I looked inside and read
I hate you.

She went to live on the Wind
River Reservation. Maybe a drop
of blood gave me courage.
I skipped on another playground
while white girls made slant eyes,
held my back like an arrow.
Mary Running Bull, I'm folding
a paper cube for you—
please look inside and see
I am your sister.

SQUID

Purplish pink, their bodies were mottled with black dots, like the fine spray twirling off a paint roller. Our fingernails peeled the skin off each mantle—as if pulling off latex, and if I was careful, it came off in one transparent piece, color suddenly faded. White flesh exposed—old squid had a slightly yellowish tinge. Fresh, a faint pink blush. Then we slid out the shells from inside the mantles, the bodies collapsing into our hands with a sigh. The inner shells were sword-shaped, reminding me of the piece of plastic inside men's shirts. My mother kept the cold water running in the sink and complained about the smell. I know it made her homesick. For me, it was the first time I understood the ocean. The scent was strong—stink of seaweed, hint of salt, metallic tang of wet stainless steel resonating against fish. And while the water whooshed and drummed into the sink, we pulled apart the tentacles from the mantle. A quick, wet suck of sound as each body separated in two. Then as if it were a tube of toothpaste, we squeezed out the mantle—entrails like cold blackberry jam. Now they were empty white pockets, and we rinsed them out, washing away the rich blackness—sumie ink off an ivory tablet. Finally, we spread open the tentacles and squeezed gently until the mouth, like a parrot's beak, snapped out. A squish accompanied by a soft, knuckle-cracking pop. We'd cut out their eyes, and sometimes I'd arrange them on the counter with beaks to look like bird faces. My fingers were rubbery and numb from the ice-cold water, and when I held them up to my nose they smelled like another country.

My mother's in geta shoes,
clopping along the driveway.
Hai. Gotchyou. Hai. I hope
the neighbors think it's kabuki.
The ants retreat into blackout
shelters soon after the first
dance. *They're smart.* She goes
inside and puts on the kettle.
I think green tea, but she pours
it into cracks and corpses
float up, legs falling off.

In gardening clothes, she hides
her black hair from the sun
in a wicker hat I wish she'd throw
away. But her voice is sweet
plum wine. In the tale of the
tongue-cut sparrow, birds turn
into beautiful women and dance
for those who are kind. They
never heard of shitakiri suzume
in this cold Wyoming town.

I'm half-and-half, and I hide
in the house, listen to my parents'
music. Outside on the pavement
a tsuzumi drum, accompanied by suzu,
temple bells, coming from their
bedroom—the chime on my father's
typewriter. Their marriage a secret,
Hiroshima's tenth anniversary.
My mother says, *Day I drop bomb.*

In Japan, they would whisper
Ai-noko, a child of passion.

But she says I'm American, though
they laughed at my eyes. Pinched
black and blue on St. Patrick's Day,
I heard her scream at my father
for not explaining things, then
she sewed me a green dress.
I'm also allergic to ants, bees,
the air I breathe. My mother
used to come inside and proudly
bare ant bites—guilty, mushroom-
shaped welts on yellow ivory.

HIROSHIMA MAIDEN

I.

My mother recognized
my feet and claimed me
at the hospital,
my face hot wax poured
into a Noh mask.
She used to chide me
for my pride
because I always
carried a parasol,
wasted money
on watermelons
to scrub my skin.
She's frightened
to look at me now
because I might see
myself in her eyes.

II.

Everybody stared
at Mrs. Roosevelt's
tea party, and I felt
a flash of shame
each time a reporter
snapped another picture.
After plastic surgery
at the American hospital
we looked like so many
rows of Q-Tips.

It was a relief not
to see each other's
faces, and our hands
began to take on
their former girlish
gestures. We almost
felt pretty again,
until one girl died
on their table. She found
the opening where they
were sewing on a new
mouth, and flew away.

III.

The other hibakusha
say I put on airs
since I came back.
I learned how to draw
on eyebrows, make
my skin all the same
color. They gave me
a wig made of real hair
that I brush down
a certain way to hide
my missing ear.
Mother tells me
not to listen,
they're only jealous,
and maybe now
I'll find a husband.
Maybe an ugly man,
though kind. But
I sour inside like
an unripe persimmon,

and every day become
stranger to myself
behind this other
person's face—a lie,
richly embroidered
by unfamiliar hands.

Part 2

HEART MOUNTAIN, 1943

I. Kimiko Ozawa

Oka-san keeps stuffing rags under
the barracks door, around cracks
in the window, to keep out smells
of snow, sage and cattle,
families pressed around us.
My feet, my mind, become numb
from standing in line all day—
lines to eat, shower, shit
in the dirty outdoor benjos.
Evenings I sweep my anger
off the barracks floor,
but the next morning it's coated
with dust, corners filled again.
Shikata ga nai, my parents keep
chanting. There is nothing
to be done. I watch
my father grow thin. Nights
he plays his shakuhachi flute,
the sound not unlike the cries
outside the barracks. The wind,
he says, takes everything.
I think this must be true.
I have taken walks inside
the barbed-wire fences,
and all the words
are pulled from my mouth.
My brothers, too, scattered
like dust. Ken fights
in the all-Nisei combat unit,
and Toji, who said No once,

No again, taken to Tule Lake.
My scalp itches and flakes, my lips,
my hands, chapped and cracked.
Sometimes I use a drop of cooking oil
to keep from blowing away.

II. Jimmy Yamamoto

Papa says we must tell the hospital
about Usagi-chan, because it's rabbit fever
season. They're exterminating,
just like they made my dog go to sleep
when we left Sacramento—he was Japanese.
And when we went to live in the stalls
at Santa Anita Racetrack, they took away
my radio so I couldn't listen to ball games,
and my camera too. How will I know if
I was really there? After that we rode
a train for three days. Mama was scared
there'd be rattlesnakes and I couldn't see
with all the shades pulled down. People
came to look at us behind barbed wire
and a pudgy girl with round eyes the color
of blue rice bowls pointed at me and said,
Why don't they look like the cartoons?
My oji-san tells a story about a rabbit,
a monkey, and a fox that lived together
in the forest. One day a hungry beggar
came and asked for help. The monkey
gathered fruit, the fox caught a big fish,
but the rabbit couldn't find anything.
So he asked them to build a fire,
and when it burned bright, tried to jump in
so he could be cooked and eaten.
The beggar was really the man-in-the-moon
and took the rabbit into the sky. Mama
and papa are asleep, and we're not supposed
to be out at night, but I'm wearing my ID tag

so I don't get put in the Lost and Found room.
I'm running as fast as I can with Usagi-chan,
and when I get to the fence there's a light
on me so round, so hot, and so yellow
I see the man-in-the-moon.

III. Masa Nakahara

I am thinking about the temple
in Nara Park. And the baby deer,
we called them, because they never
got big, never lost their spots.
I used to feed them bites
of osembei, though my oka-san
told me it would make them sick.
My son George, his picture
was in the paper yesterday:
*Nisei Interpreters Quiz Jap
Prisoner.* The picture was so fuzzy,
hard to tell who was who.
They looked like kids to me—
like my sister's boys
in Japan. Mostly I think about
the deer during blackout tests,
when we're told to *Make
Park County the blackest spot
in the nation.* Yesterday
I gathered wild mustard grass
to make tsukemono—sprinkled
damp greens with salt,
put them in a large bowl,
squeezed down with a plate,
a rock. The pickles tasted
so good, earth and brine,
they made my mouth burn.
George always liked hot dogs.
I used to serve them over rice
with shoyu, and he'd say,

No Ma, that's not the way
you're supposed to eat them.
I dreamed I saw him crouched
in front of the shrine
at the temple in Nara Park.
He held a spotted deer
in his arms. It was kicking,
and he whispered name, rank, and
serial number in its ear.

IV. Chester Korematsu

Fish are heavier than coal.
Maybe you wouldn't think so
the way they scoot like mercury
underwater, slide into a ball
of tossed silver as the net's
pulled in. But try and lift
them into a boat. Since
I'm not used to people
I took a graveyard shift
heaving coal. Forty-five tons
a night, I like knowing camp
will be a little bit warmer
the next day. Besides, I
scare most of the kids since
Sab Sakai stuck a fork
in my eye for nagging him.
Maybe I did. We'd stolen
supplies from the mess hall,
made ourselves home brew.
The tough kids, though,
aren't afraid, follow me
around and call me Daruma-san,
say they'll give back my eye
for the sweets in my pocket.
I show them how to mend nets,
set bait. Michiko
never liked Terminal Island.
My Japanese isn't too good
and I don't know for sure
what she was saying

that day she stood
on the deck and stared
at the fish flopping around
her feet. I think maybe
she said she was choking.
Or lonely. I guess
I talked so much to her picture
that by the time she
arrived I'd run out of words.
At least she's safe, home
in Nagasaki again. I am glad
she didn't see them take away
my boat, glad she wasn't here
when I found the baby
someone left in a coal bin.
You get used to things, though.
I even found a fish fossil
once, keep it in a cigar box
with Michiko's picture, and
joined the fire department.
The place is a big tinderbox
and I like being caught
between flames and water.

V. Lily Iwasaki

Minoru, it's been over a month
since they took you to Tule Lake
and it makes me frostbitten inside.
Papa calls you No-No Boys bad names.
I think he's burning your letters.
You should've seen the way
he shushed grandmother
when she spoke Japanese
on the bus in downtown Cody.
Alice Fujioka got so big she
couldn't come to school anymore,
and three days ago someone
found a dead baby frozen
to the bottom of a coal bin.
Dough-faced Mrs. Corbett,
who I call oni-baba
behind her back, demonstrates
spot removal in Home Economics,
how to make over
our shabby old clothes.
I was born in the year of the tiger
so I've been told to make belts
of 1,000 stitches for the 442nd
to protect them from enemy bullets.
With red, unbroken thread,
I stitch and knot seventeen times,
one for each year of my life,
pass it on to the next girl.
Minoru, do you remember seeing
"Arctic Thrills" at the mess hall,

how we left early
and you taught me
to blow smoke rings
with your Lucky Strikes?
You said the sky here
looked like the planetarium
in Los Angeles, and we promised
to meet at Star Festival
like Orihime and Kengyu.
I'm so scared, Minoru, I heard
twenty people were shot at Tule Lake.
And so I stole some white fabric,
red thread to make a charm belt
for you. No one will help me.
But even caged, a tiger's
full of rage and cunning.

VI. Sam Toyama

Mother held up a wrinkled fashion
magazine as if it smelled bad,
while Mayumi frowned and snipped.
I picked up Keiko's hair,
fanned it through my fingers,
glistening like a crow's wing.
Then we scrubbed the place down,
and even though it was below zero,
opened the door and window
so the evil spirits could leave.
I couldn't stop laughing
and Keiko pinched me. Before
the New Year's Eve dance,
she made me draw stocking seams
up the curve of her calves
with an ink pen. Outside
the mess hall, wind whipped
her bare legs and her shoes filled
with snow. I took them off
and cupped her icy toes in my hands.
She'd sewn a bit of lace at the cuffs
and collar of her dress
to make it prettier, she told me,
and the twirl of her skirt,
prickle of eyelashes against
my cheek almost made me forget
soldiers stationed in watchtowers
with rifles. Keiko doesn't know
about the insomnia, how I
stand guard over her,

waiting to tend my mother's cough.
I may be drafted soon,
but Keiko won't hear of it.
She covers her ears, swears
at me in rapid-fire Japanese.
And as I lie here with my cheek
pressed against her stomach,
I don't know anymore
if it's hope or disillusion I feel
kicking me in the face inside her.

VII. Nina Inoue

Since the shoe ration, I can't play
with Kathy Kawamura. She's in Block 25
and mama says I'll wear out my soles.
She never says anything to grandmother,
who goes to the latrine in Block 18
where they have partitions. Before,
it was my job to unfold a cardboard
Purex box and hold it up like a screen.
Her head stuck out over the Purex label,
but everyone made their eyes glassy
like they didn't recognize anybody.
The walls between apartments don't go
to the ceilings. At night, my sister
and I can hear old Mrs. Noguchi snoring
real loud on one side, and the Tanakas
screaming at each other in Japanese
on the other. Sometimes they even
throw things, and once we listened
to them make funny hoo-hooing sounds
like owls when they stopped fighting.
It's hard not to gawk at them and giggle
in the mess line, but mama always
gives us stink-eye, so we bow instead.
Once a week after school I take lessons
from Mr. Yoshimura, who was a concert
pianist in San Francisco. He hides
his frostbitten hands in gloves.
Mama told me not to ask him why.
I had to play in a recital and we sent
for a yellow dress in the mail-order

catalogue. But when it finally arrived
the ruffles were only sewn on the front
where you could see them in the picture.
I stamped my feet and cried, but mama
made me play anyway. Everyone,
even Mrs. Tanaka, said how pretty
I looked in my dress, and that's when
I learned what it means to be kind.

VIII. Yoshio Miyake

It sours my incense, disturbs the sleep
of my ancestors, the clattering tin lids
they use to wake us in the mornings.
What kind of way is this to begin a day?
Take a vacation, gramps, they told me.
I am Issei. But now I am the guardian
of horned toads. The first one I found
on a walk—some mischievous boys pulled
off her tail. I chased them with my stick,
brought her home. Her tail grew back,
she became mother to four toads the size
of nickels. Soon people from clear across
camp were bringing them to my door. I built
little wooden barracks on my porch.
Boarding houses and a maternity ward.
I filled them with sand, put in rocks,
planted sagebrush. All morning long,
sometimes for six hours, I gather live ants.
Only black ones—the red ones bite back.
I have seen dry carcasses with the eyes
eaten out beside ant hills. These I take
away, bury along the edge of the cemetery.
Squatting by the mounds of earth, I scoop
ants up with a spoon and shake them into
a glass jar. Some evenings, my grandson
brings over his friends. Today the boys
are happy. They say the American hero
Superman was looking for Jap saboteurs
in the camps but didn't find any.
Who this Superman? I ask. They show me

drawings of someone wearing a red blanket
tied around his neck. Baka! We take
the internees out on leave, enjoy their
wide, smiling mouths, creamy bellies,
the rows of spines along their backs.
I show them how to stroke the rough heads—
forehead to horns, until they nestle down
flat in my hand, hooded eyes lidding shut.
Now all the boys want to try. I warn them
to be gentle and show respect, or the toads
will suddenly wake, eyes spitting blood.

IX. Chikako Okano

I know tweezing away dead skin
from the kitchen helper's face
before laying on fresh gauze
hurts him, but he doesn't flinch.
Arigato gozai-masu, he whispers
from behind the bandages when
I'm finished. He was broiling
meat fats to make soap for the camp
when the oven door blew open.
Your face will be like new
I want so much to tell him.
Last month the watchtower guards
brought in a little boy found
tangled in barbed wire the way
antelope sometimes get caught.
He trembled all night.
On New Year's Eve a man walked
all the way to the hospital
from Bachelors' Quarters
with a fork in his eye,
apologized for the late hour.
An Issei woman died tonight
from a bleeding stomach ulcer
even after four orderlies and I
gave blood for a transfusion.
I think of how she'll be buried
in Heart Mountain Cemetery
with my cells inside,
how her bones will lock
into ice, melt into spring

when the Stinking Water River
thaws. I think of how
this place eats us all up.
My shift ends before dawn
and I go to the ice pond, skate
on crazy, reckless blades
and sing into the wind:
Poison mushrooms, tularemia,
rattlesnakes, pneumonia.
The man from maintenance crew
trails after me, cleaving away
the scars I leave behind.

X. Minoru Saito

When I shaved my head and became
a No-No Boy, papa said I'd shamed
the entire family. I wasn't his son,
but a ghost, and he quit going
to Saturday night shoji games,
didn't even want to show his face.
And I'll never be able to explain
to him I just couldn't get his car
out of my head. That black Packard
sedan with gray plush upholstery
and push-button radio that always
made my mother's mouth scrunch up
it cost so much money. Sundays
he'd close the produce store early,
buff and polish that car until
it glistened like mama's lacquer
tea tray, put on his best suit
and make the family go for a ride.
But we never went faster than ten
miles an hour, the other cars
honking, passing, fists shaking,
mama's eyes straight ahead,
hands neatly folded on her beaded
clutch purse, my sister squealing
Go faster in embarrassment. Papa,
oblivious, would just tip his hat
and wave. When the evacuation orders
came, no one had the guts to ask
what he was going to do about
the car. The morning we left

he finally sold it for twenty bucks.
It was the best offer. *Funny car
for a Jap to have,* the man said
as he drove away, and my mother
had to stop papa from burning
the twenty-dollar bill. Papa,
it was his Packard, not yours,
that made me say No.

Part 3

SONGS FOR AN APPROACHING

RAINY SEASON

I.

Today the tomatoes will blush
outside my door—
skin the color of young jade

glazed orange in
the last firing of summer's kiln.
But I sleep through

the afternoon, left eye a bruised
ache of sinus,
asthmatic wheeze of floorboards over

my head. Sirens
sing the tornado home to me—
clicking my toes

until the cyclone's eye blinks open
in surprise. See
the late-blooming iris on my nightstand

open her mouth,
invite me to swim down her cool
green length of throat?

II.

Wind blows its fat-cheeked trumpet riff,
skittering leaves
up against my door at night while

the cat curls into
my armpit—wrapped nose to tail, neat
as a croissant,

and my chilled fingers greedily
skim the yeasty
rise of his side, buttery glaze

of yellow fur.
Tomorrow I'll pluck wilted buds
from the ivy

geranium and feel remorse
for parched branches
straining toward the windowpane

and rain, beyond,
that quiets maple leaves, matted
against asphalt

like shreds of red and orange silk.
And when I walk
to the store for a newspaper,

I'll keep saying
to myself the word *wisteria,*
as my feet pull

scraps of color from the pavement's
skin, revealing
leaf prints etched in black mold, like

the pattern of
a kimono found burned into
a woman after

Hiroshima, and it is almost
too beautiful,
too horrible for me to bear.

III.

This mute cocooning is something
less than grief but
more than blue—leaves me wondering

where sweetness goes
once tomatoes fall from their vines
and start their rot,

slithering out of the yellow skins
that litter my yard
like burst party balloons. Why does

rain's monologue
override my tongue even though
its language is strange?

But maybe silence is song, so
I keep it furled
tight around me like the ornate

origami
of a peony bud, and wait
for spring to come—

for the delicate fingers of ants
to burrow in
and pry each of my petals loose.

THE WOMAN WHO LOVES INSECTS

If you stand outside my gate
   and peer between the slats
you might see me in the shrubs,

gathering up the caterpillars
   who disguise themselves
as bird-droppings, to tuck into

my kimono sleeves. I will not be
   the kind who makes pets
of butterflies. They only leave

a glitter of dust on my palm
   that makes me sneeze,
and they climb at night inside

my rice-paper lanterns, quick
   as I can snap my fingers,
explode into a curl of bitter-

smelling incense. (Even Buddha
   would wrinkle his nose.)
And if you take care not to

trample the garden beetles, tear
   the spider's glistening veil,
you may come up to my window

and leave me a token—a snail,
   a locust, a cockroach.
I know the dragonfly's song,

the war-cries of grass-crickets,
   and will sing them to you
through a chink in the blinds.

And if my favorite caterpillar
   should accidentally drop
from my kimono sleeve and brush

past your face—and you do not
   let him break open
against the pebbles, but unfold

your fan in time to catch
   his fall—then I
will be the praying mantis,

who wears a mask on her wings
   to scare off birds.
I will pull away the mantle

from my face, and if you
   are not afraid of my fierce
eyebrows, my disheveled hair,

my unblackened teeth that give me
   a white, barbaric grin,
I will feed you tender leaves,

nestle and stroke you in the palm
   of my hand until you
are plump with nectar. Kawamushi,

my hairy caterpillar.

My honeybee.

My centipede.

STAR FESTIVAL

I. Sumida River

Rice-paper lanterns bob
like sake-flushed faces,
drowsy old men, and the river
makes my ukata sleeves flutter.
Hand-painted fans slice
the heat, and chilled sushi
disappears into my mouth
from ivory chopsticks.
As the crowd of rented boats
nudge each other music
becomes confused—geisha
strumming her shamisen,
a kabuki actor singing.
Soon the firework artists,
Tamaya and Kagiya,
will have their contest—
thunder of geta shoes pounding
the sides of the boats
in judgment.

II. Orihime's Song

I came from mulberry trees
where farmers lined wooden
trays with fragrant straw.
A weaver girl, singing
to the sharp claps of shuttle,
drumming treadle, I made
silk cloth of worm thread.
But when you came, my loom

fell silent, we made love in
mulberry groves, intoxicated
as birds eating fermented
berries. And when the gods
watched us, they were jealous,
threw two stars into the sky.
I burn alone, but know you
feel my warmth, understand.
And for this one night I am
a woman and you will row across
the Milky Way to me. Impatient
to feel your fingers touch
my face, your mouth drink me,
to have you inside me again.

III. A Thousand Cranes

I go to the bamboo grove,
cut down a young tree
to set in front of my house.
For days I fold
rice paper cranes,
a thousand.
I string them together
with silk thread,
tie them onto the tree.
I write a tanka, a wish,
roll it into a scroll,
place it at the very top.
I am selfish.

PEONY LANTERN

Do not forget me.
Once I was woman, but now flesh
is mere sleight-of-hand,

illusion to a
willing eye. So you must call me
back with apricots,

incense, and bitter
fragrant tea made from leaves and stems
of tender spring twigs.

Remember to raise
bright orbs of rice-paper lanterns
by the goldfish pond,

so they can watch for me
with the yellow, unblinking gaze
of nocturnal things,

and set free your jars
of fireflies, spraying clouds of sparks,
so they will cluster

at the hems of my
kimono sleeves and guide the way.
Remember my name,

Tsuyu, morning dew,
and I will appear, carrying
a peony lantern

whose pink glow
disguises wildness in my eyes, warms
the chill of my hands.

Forgive me. I have no feet—
no geta shoes to echo against the bridge,
no footprints when I leave.

Do not forget me.
Or the heavy braid of hair I pull
across your thigh will

crumble into ash,
my arms will no longer hold you,
and in the morning

you will find only
the delicate bones of my fingers
curved around your neck.

Once, when I was a girl,
I kept a cricket in a bamboo
cage, to sing for me

at night. I was careless,
I didn't feed her, and so she ate
her own limbs, one by one.

UTOYASUKATA

My heart's a black bird.
I bury its fever
in cool grains of sand
beneath a tangle of willows
and forget where I put it.
I'm the only one who knows
its name, so I wait
for night and call Uto.
It hears my cry
and calls back Yasukata.
I stuff its gullet
with morsels of dream.

Tonight there's no reply
and I find you instead
with a hibachi grill, a clump
of black down, a beak
and two scrawny claws.
You've been spying on me
and the smell in the air
delicious—shoyu, ginger,
sugar, and bird flesh.
You know my tears
are blood, they burn,
and you protect yourself
with a large hat, a raincoat.

Take them off. Be naked
and let my hunger beat
you until your insides
flutter at my voice.
Uto, I'll whisper,
and you'll say Yasukata.

PEONY LOVER

A thinnest sliver of moon, and caterpillars
gather in their bodies
with the wiry, circular precision

of a rice-paper lantern
folding back down on itself, colored
patterns collapsing into

denser, indecipherable forms. Rabbits
leave lacy teethmarks
rimming the ragged edges of lettuce,

and I am like the opossum
who stares up with glowing, hungry eyes
waiting for persimmons to fall.

All night tree frogs throb and thrum
with the numbing pulse
of a discotheque, and fat, lacquer-backed

cockroaches creep in shiny,
bumper-to-bumper lines toward the promise
of food, drawing a zigzag

connect-a-dot from garbage can to can,
hub to hub, the way your flight
now circles another city, talons outstretched,

like a blinking, red-eyed
bird, while the damp of your sweat fades
from my pillowcase.

Because I let your hands undo me
like an origami crane,
fold by fold, fingers easing out creases,

because I let the ink
of your brushstrokes seep the whiteness
of my paper-thin skin

and mark me, I could call this love,
or maybe delusion.
And when I creep barefoot in moonlight

with my hair undone,
reach into the sky to pull you back down,
there is nothing

but heat, and sound, and dizziness,
only a handful
of peony petals crumpling in my fists.

ODE TO SUSHI

The gleaming arc
of knife
behind the counter
smooth as Buddha's
belly.
Two fingers full
of vinegared rice
slapping
into the cup
of a palm.
Octopus legs
in suctioned slivers
grip my tongue.
Seaweed, sugary eel,
fattest tuna,
silvery mackerel,
yellowtail
more tender,
ephemeral,
than a labial kiss.
I'm hungry
and want more.

Horseradish
makes me flush,
strips of pink ginger
to cleanse
the palate,
like pulling up
cellophane
on a magic slate,
the orange insides

of a sea urchin
cushioned as a womb.
Mirugai,
the giant white clam,
frilled and crisp
as a petticoat.

Salmon roe
lines my teeth
like rubies,
burst in my mouth—
salty beads
of pomegranate.
A raw quail's egg,
color of goldenrod
slides
down my throat
into my stomach,
where tides
begin to ebb,
where the sound
of beating wings
sigh on the horizon,
where my navel
rises
a white moon.

FISH WIFE

The sting of the hook in my lip,
fluttering gills,
and then the parched, awful burning

as I was pulled
up and torn through the roof of one life
into another,

where the lovely rainbow of my skin
congealed to slime
while between thumb and forefinger

you spread the webbing
of my fins, measured my twisting
weight in the palm

of your hand, then dipped me back in
to the cool balm
of my familiar realm, to quiver

for one moment
of surprise, my tail unfurling,
before I darted

away. But I had seen too much
already, and so
I returned to repay your kindness

in the disguise
of a woman, with hands and feet
and hair, a blue

iridescent kimono, let you take
me for your wife,
and for awhile, you didn't seem

to mind when I
lunged at dragonflies, or nibbled
on the creamy,

vanilla edges of gardenias.
Who can tell what
makes a man become suspicious?

I knew that you'd
begun to spy when you refused
to eat my soup,

the one you used to think was
so delicious.
You hid in the rafters, watched me

crumble beanpaste,
grind out a nutty fragrance from
sesame seeds

with a mortar and a pestle,
cut out carrots
into the shape of plum blossoms,

lift my robes to
urinate into the soup pot
so you could have

the best of my fresh, brothy stock.
Before I left
I gave you a lacquerware box

so heavy you'd think
it would be worth my weight in gold.
I packed it

full of earth worms and damsel flies,
bumblebee wings,
and gleaming coils of fine, silk twine.

KAKITSUBATA

Come to the place of eight bridges
where streams ribbon
around thickets of ghost-bamboo

like the nine tails
of a gleaming, silver-tailed fox.
Come when the moon

has been polished to the creamy
yellow of old
ivory, and black wisps of cloud

give it a strange,
mask-like tilt in the sky—perhaps
for a moment

you suddenly remember the face
of a woman
you once loved. Come down to the marsh

where iris blooms
so I can emerge in my human
form, blossoming

limb by petal, petal to limb
and dance for you,
because sometimes, I am lonely.

I can tell you
poems so sad the tears will sting
your eyes like bees,

and if I should accidentally
blind you, I'll cut
out the liver of my pet rabbit,

feed it to you
in slices thin as fresh sashimi,
and give you sight

again by sacrifice. Come closer,
lift up the haze
of veil from my face, stare deep down

my purple gaze
and let your tongue be drawn into
the intricate

pollen and nectar of my mouth.
Let me keep you
here, since I cannot let myself

be torn away—
the bottom hem of my gown is lined
with mud, my toes

are pale and tender as straw mushrooms.
Stay for awhile
and I will show you a secret.

If you scatter
fresh camellia leaves on the ground,
fill them with wine,

thirsty sparrows will become drunk
and sleep there. Stay
just until morning, when the sun's

heat curls the leaves,
wrapping up the sleeping sparrows
like little gifts.

Take them home with you, build them
bamboo cages,
and when you think I'm only a dream

you had one night,
the song of sparrows will always tell
you otherwise.

ACKNOWLEDGMENTS

These poems first appeared in the following publications:

"Chrysanthemums," *American Identities: Contemporary Multicultural Voices,* ed. Robert Pack and Jay Parini (Hanover and London: Middlebury College Press, 1994).

"A Dance of Wooden Shoes," *Crab Orchard Review* 3, no. 1 (fall/winter 1997).

"Fish Wife," *Black Warrior Review* 22, no. 2 (spring/summer 1996).

"Heart Mountain, 1943," *Parnassus: Poetry in Review* 20, nos. 1–2 (Twentieth Anniversary Issue, 1995).

"Hiroshima Maiden," *Seneca Review* 25, no. 2 (fall 1995).

"Kakitsubata," *Phoebe* 25 (winter/summer 1996).

"Ningyo," *American Identities: Contemporary Multicultural Voices,* ed. Robert Pack and Jay Parini (Hanover and London: Middlebury College Press, 1994).

"Ode to Sushi," *Crab Orchard Review* 3, no. 1 (fall/winter 1997).

"Oyurushi," *Alligator Juniper* (fall 1997).

"Pearls," *New England Review* 16, no. 2 (spring 1994).

"Peony Lover," *Breeze* 2, no. 1 (January–February 1996).

"Squid," *Crab Orchard Review* 3, no. 1 (fall/winter 1997).

"The Woman Who Loves Insects," *Cream City Review* 19, no. 1 (spring 1995).